Kate Middleton

Duchess of Cambridge

First published in 2014 by Wayland

Copyright © Wayland 2014

Wayland
338 Euston Road
London
NW1 3BH

Wayland Australia
Level 17/207 Kent Street
Sydney NSW 2000

Senior editor: Julia Adams

Produced for Wayland by Dynamo
Written by Hettie Bingham

Picture acknowledgements:
Key: b=bottom, t=top, r=right, l=left, m=middle, bgd=background

Alamy: p5 tr, p26 bl Adrian Dennis. **Shutterstock:** Backgrounds and
doodles: casejustin, Studio DMM Photography, Designs & Art, blue67design,
Belodarova Kseniya, Ohn Mar, alicedaniel, Aleks Melnik, Maaike Boot, Dooder,
karen roach, Incomible, Inga Linder, pinoyo, Marrvid, bioraven, M_A_R_G_O,
Nanna Studio P1 m Featureflash; p2 tl art-TAyga; p2 bl andersphoto; p5
br Stephen Finn; p6 m Elaine Barker; p8/9 m Alexander Ryabintsev; p10 tl
Cidonia; p11 tl cosma; p12 bl Mega Pixel; p13 tl Gurgen BAkhshetsyan; p13
tr Guido Amrein, Switzerland; p16 ml Mr Pics; 18 br Mr Pics; p18/19 m Elaine
Barker; p20 bl Featureflash; p21 bl Featureflash; p20/21 m Liskus; p22/23 bgd
ildogesto; p22 tr Artgraphixel; p23 tr Globe Turner; p23 l julinzy; p23 ml Globe
Turner; p23 mr megastocker; p23 r Globe Turner; p24 mr Featureflash; p25
m Iryna Dobrovynska; p27 tl Juriah Mosin; p29 br Mr Pics. **Splash News:** P2
m Weir Photos; p5 bl Weir Photos; p6 bm The Middleton Family; p7 m Simon
Hammond; p8 tr Simon Hammond; p8 bl Tony Clark; p13 bl The Middleton
Family; p14/15 m The Middleton Family; p19 m Allpix; p21 m Weir Photos;
p25 bl Weir Photos. **Getty:** p1 Adrian Dennis; p2, p22, p29, p4 WPA Pool, p5
Ben Stansall. **iStock:** p7 br ac_bnphotos; p11 tr EdStock; p17 b EdStock; p20 tr
EdStock2; p23 br EdStock2; p26 mr EdStock2; p30 tr EdStock2.

Dewey classification: 941'.086'092-dc23

ISBN 978 0 7502 8261 1
E-book ISBN 978 0 7502 8 7760
Printed in China
10 9 8 7 6 5 4 3 2 1

Wayland is a division of Hachette Children's Books,
an Hachette UK company.
www.hachette.co.uk

Kate Middleton

Contents

Kate, Duchess of Cambridge

Today's Princess

Duchess, charity patron, ambassador, style icon, wife, mother of a future king and all round hard-working royal: Kate Middleton is a thoroughly modern princess. Her subtle mix of serene dignity, glamour and warmth attracts admiration from the people of nations the world over.

NAME: Catherine, Duchess of Cambridge (formerly Catherine Elizabeth Middleton, known as Kate)

TITLES: Her Royal Highness the Duchess of Cambridge, Countess of Strathearn and Lady Carrickfergus. She could also be known as HRH Princess William of Wales if she chose.

BORN: 9 January 1982

EDUCATION: St Andrew's School, Buckhold; Marlborough College, Wiltshire; St Andrew's University, Fife, Scotland

DEGREE: 2:1 MA (Hons) degree in History of Art

HOMETOWN: Bradfield Southend, Berkshire and Chapel Row near Newbury, Berkshire

RESIDENCES: Kensington Palace

Husband, Prince William

St Andrews University Building, Scotland

Kate as a Kid

Kate's childhood was similiar to that of many little girls – she loved going to Brownies, attending birthday parties and dressing-up in fancy costumes.

Catherine Elizabeth Middleton was born on 9 January 1982 at the Royal Berkshire Hospital in Reading. Later that year she was christened at St Andrew's Church, Bradfield, Berkshire, where the family lived. She did not have to wait long for the company of her younger sister, Philippa, who was born in September 1983. Their brother, James, was born in 1987 and that completed the Middleton family.

DID YOU KNOW?

Kate went to Brownies at St Andrew's Church where she and her brother and sister were also christened.

Amman, Jordan.

When she was just two years old, Kate's parents moved to Amman, Jordan, where they worked for British Airways. Whilst there, she attended an English-language nursery school. The family moved back to Berkshire in 1986 when Kate was four.

Kate's first home in England was a semi-detached house in the village of Bradfield Southend, Berkshire. Kate lived there until she was 13 years old when the family moved to Ashampstead Common. The new house was larger and had out-buildings where her parents ran their party-supply business.

Kate loved party bags as a child. She once said that she enjoyed:

'anything that Mummy would normally never allow me to have. They were always such a treat.'

Mrs Middleton's skills as a party supplier came in handy when her own children had birthdays. Kate has happy memories of her childhood parties. When asked about the perfect party, she remembered dressing up in a 'pair of clown dungarees … They were white with big red spots and … a small hula hoop for the waistband – genius!'

MY FAVOURITE PARTY MEMORY OF ALL IS THE AMAZING WHITE RABBIT MARSHMALLOW CAKE THAT MUMMY MADE WHEN I WAS SEVEN.

Kate's favourite party food was:

'definitely jelly. Every time I have it now it reminds me of my childhood.'

Kate's Family

Kate is the first commoner to marry into the royal family. Nobody in her family was **titled**; in fact, her parents came from very ordinary beginnings.

Michael Middleton, Catherine's father, was born in Leeds and is the son of a pilot. He worked for British Airways first as a flight attendant and then as a flight dispatcher. When Party Pieces became successful, Michael left British Airways to join the family firm.

Carole Middleton, formerly Goldsmith, grew up in a council flat in Southall, West London, where she attended the local state school. She became a flight attendant and worked for British Airways alongside her husband. In 1987, Carole founded a mail order company called Party Pieces that sells party supplies and decorations. The business became a success and made the Middletons wealthy.

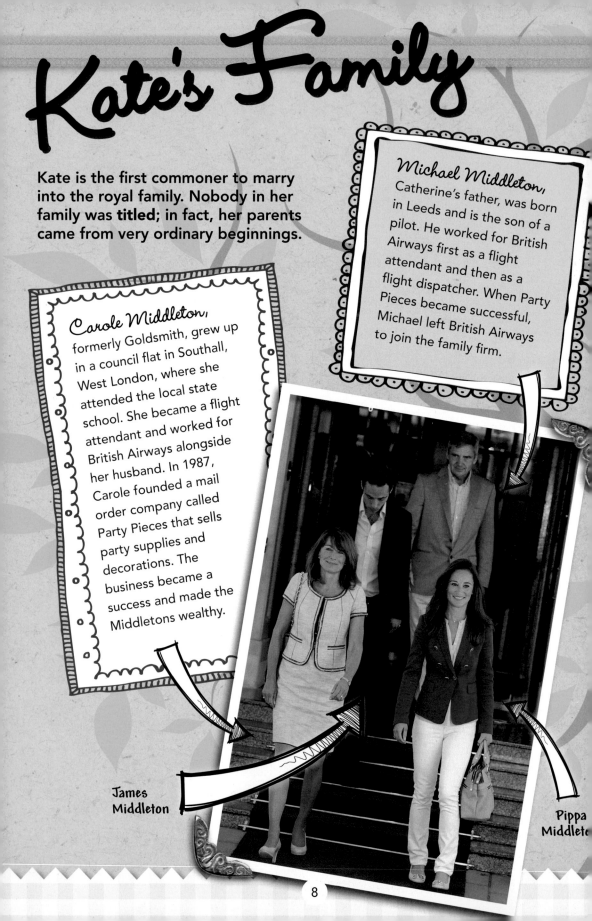

James Middleton

Pippa Middleton

Pippa Middleton is Kate's younger sister. She graduated from the University of Edinburgh with an English degree. She went on to work in public relations and then as a party planner. She became a bit of a celebrity after she was Kate's maid of honour at her wedding, and now lives her life in the public eye. Pippa is the author of *Celebrate*, a book on party planning. She has also written articles for publications including *The Spectator* and *Vanity Fair*.

James Middleton is Kate's younger brother. He began studying for a degree in environmental resources management at the University of Edinburgh, but left before he had finished in order to set up his own business. Following in his mother's footsteps, James's business is the Cake Kit Company. It makes novelty cakes which are sold through the Middletons' company, Party Pieces. He also supplies baking kits for home bakers to make their own novelty cakes. James has been open about the fact that he is **dyslexic** and often speaks in pubic to raise awareness of the condition.

THE MIDDLETON FAMILY COAT OF ARMS

In 2011, Michael Middleton was granted a family coat of arms by the College of Arms. The background of the Middleton shield is divided into two colours, red and blue. There is a gold chevron in the centre of the shield that represents Kate's mother's maiden name – Goldsmith. There are also three acorns on the shield. These are symbolic of England and also a feature of west Berkshire, where the Middleton family have made their family home.

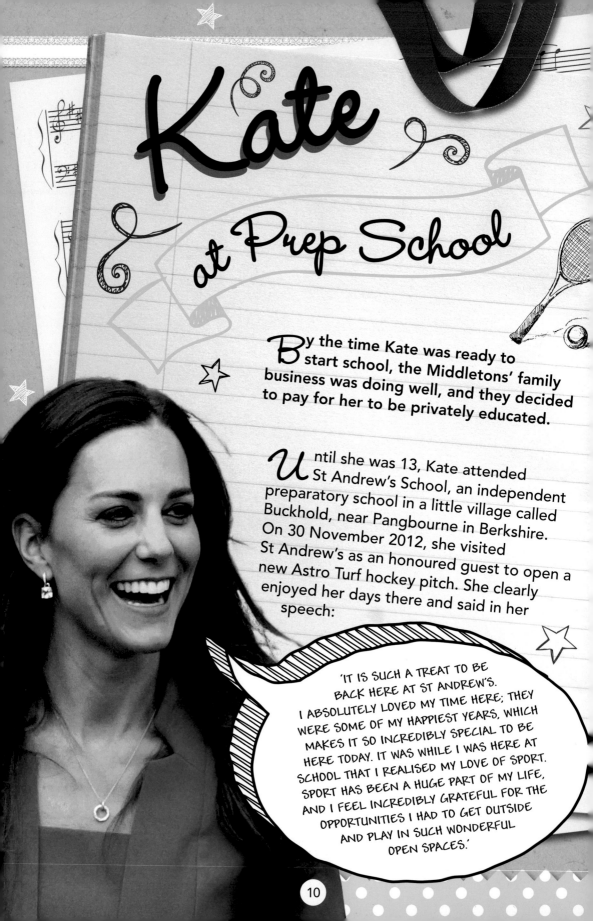

Kate
at Prep School

By the time Kate was ready to start school, the Middletons' family business was doing well, and they decided to pay for her to be privately educated.

Until she was 13, Kate attended St Andrew's School, an independent preparatory school in a little village called Buckhold, near Pangbourne in Berkshire. On 30 November 2012, she visited St Andrew's as an honoured guest to open a new Astro Turf hockey pitch. She clearly enjoyed her days there and said in her speech:

'IT IS SUCH A TREAT TO BE BACK HERE AT ST ANDREW'S. I ABSOLUTELY LOVED MY TIME HERE; THEY WERE SOME OF MY HAPPIEST YEARS, WHICH MAKES IT SO INCREDIBLY SPECIAL TO BE HERE TODAY. IT WAS WHILE I WAS HERE AT SCHOOL THAT I REALISED MY LOVE OF SPORT. SPORT HAS BEEN A HUGE PART OF MY LIFE, AND I FEEL INCREDIBLY GRATEFUL FOR THE OPPORTUNITIES I HAD TO GET OUTSIDE AND PLAY IN SUCH WONDERFUL OPEN SPACES.'

Kate

Kate was indeed very keen on sport and, while at St Andrew's, she excelled at many games including tennis, hockey, netball and rounders. She was also a talented swimmer and athlete, winning a school cup for 'outstanding overall sporting achievement'.

Kate also had a talent for music; she played the flute and sang in the chapel choir. She was once commended in a BBC carol competition. Before leaving the school, Kate had passed her grade three flute exam with **merit** and also her grade five in singing.

DID YOU KNOW?

Kate had the nickname Squeak at school. The school had two guinea pigs – one called Pip and one called Squeak. As one of the guinea pigs had the same name as Pippa, everyone decided to call Kate Squeak after the other guinea pig!

Kate at College

Kate's secondary education was at Marlborough College, a co-educational boarding school in Wiltshire, where she spent many happy years.

'She was just like any other girl at the school ... ordinary, hard-working, athletic and easy-going'.
— Charlie Leslie, fellow pupil

'I don't think you'd find anyone in Marlborough with a bad word to say about her. She excelled in all her subjects and was an A-grade pupil across the board.'
— Marlborough College master

After leaving Marlborough College in 2000, Kate was offered a place at Edinburgh University. However, she decided to turn this down and take a gap year instead. During this year, Kate made use of her time by planning trips abroad to broaden her horizons.

FLORENCE, Italy

FLORENCE, Italy

The first part of Kate's gap year was spent in Florence. Here, she took a course in Italian language and arts at the British Institute in Palazzo dello Strozzino.

PATAGONIA, Chile

Later, Kate joined a 10-week Raleigh International expedition to Patagonia in Chile. By coincidence, Prince William had been on a similar expedition the previous October. They had both been looked after by the same expedition leader, Malcolm Sutherland. Speaking later about this strange coincidence, he said:

'WITH THE EXPEDITION THAT WILLIAM WAS ON, THERE WAS A CLEAR UNDERSTANDING OF WHO HE WAS, WHILE KATE WAS LIKE YOU AND I.'

Kate applied and was offered a place at St Andrews University in Fife, Scotland, to study History of Art. She began her course in 2001 and it was here that she first met Prince William, who started in the same year to study a joint honours degree in History of Art and Geography. With some of their lectures overlapping and rooms in the same hall of residence, it is little wonder that the pair soon became friends.

Kate graduated from St Andrews in 2005 with a 2:1 MA (Hons) degree in History of Art.

Romance

Kate and Prince William began their relationship as friends, but somewhere along the way they fell in love.

Kate and William had a lot in common: their love of sport and the shared experience of their expeditions in Chile. Having become close friends in their second year at St Andrews, they shared a flat with fellow friends and students Fergus Boyd and Olivia Bleasdale.

'HE IS VERY LUCKY TO BE GOING OUT WITH ME.'

Some say that it was Kate's appearance in a university fashion show that captured William's heart. Whatever it was, sometime during their second year at university, Kate and Prince William became more than just friends. For their last two years at St Andrews, they rented a cottage with their old flat mates. It was a little way out of town, so they had more privacy. Importantly, this gave the couple space and time to get to know each other even better.

By 2004, it was confirmed that the couple were dating and the eyes of the world were upon them. Kate managed to remain calm and dignified, despite the pressures she was suddenly facing. She also displayed a quick wit. Once, when somebody commented that she was lucky to be going out with Prince William, she immediately replied:

'He is very lucky to be going out with me.'

William began to visit Kate's family in Berkshire and is said to have enjoyed the relaxed atmosphere, with plenty of easy chatter and clatter in the warm family kitchen. It was a far cry from the life that William was used to.

Meanwhile, Kate was getting to know William's family too. She once said:
'I was quite nervous about meeting William's father, but he was very, very welcoming and very friendly.'

Kate soon got a taste of William's world. Such was the interest in her relationship with the prince that she was followed by the press for months on end. There were journalists camped outside her apartment day and night. Everyone wanted to know if Prince William was going to pop the question and ask Kate to be his wife.

Understandably, the pressure was extremely hard on both William and Kate, and in 2007 they split up. They didn't stay apart for long though – they were clearly unhappy without each other. Kate and William have both said that this time apart gave them the chance to think about what they wanted. And what they really wanted turned out to be each other.

Engagement

William proposed to Kate nine years after they had first met. Both the public and the two families were delighted by the news.

Kate Middleton and Prince William announced their engagement on 16 November 2010.

The couple had been away on holiday in Kenya with friends when William proposed to Kate.

'We had been talking about marriage for a while, so it wasn't a massively big surprise, but I took her out somewhere nice and proposed'

said William.

As the couple were holidaying with friends, the proposal took Kate unawares:

'I really didn't expect it at all,'

she said after the announcement.

'It was very romantic'

she added.

It is traditional for a man to ask his intended's father for her hand in marriage. William decided not to do this,

'I was afraid he might say no,' he joked. But he revealed that he did speak to Kate's dad, referring to him as 'Mike', soon afterwards and that everything has been alright.

Talking about taking on a role in the royal family, Kate said:

'I really hope I can make a difference, even in the smalles way. I'm looking forward to helping as much as I can.'

Kate's engagement ring is rather special as it is the same engagement ring that was worn by Princess Diana, William's mother. It is a large sapphire surrounded by diamonds. William had been carrying it around in his rucksack for three weeks before he proposed!

Referring to his mother, William explained:

'She's not going to be around to share in the fun and excitement of it all. This was my way of keeping her close to it all.'

Princess Diana died in 1997 as the result of a car accident.

Friends of William and Kate say that their love for each other has built up over a long period of time. It is a relationship based on close friendship.

The Wedding

On 29 April 2011

Kate and William

became husband and wife.

They also acquired new titles, becoming the

Duke and Duchess of Cambridge.

It was the day that the nation had waited for: the royal wedding. It was declared a public holiday and across the United Kingdom and around the Commonwealth and beyond, people celebrated by throwing street parties. Whole communities and people from all walks of life came together to join in the fun.

The ceremony took place at Westminster Abbey in London. The marriage was conducted by the Archbishop of Canterbury, Rowan Williams. The service was broadcast live and millions of people watched as the happy couple made their vows. A global audience of 72 million people watched the wedding on YouTube and, in the United Kingdom alone, more than 36 million watched it happen on television.

As Prince William is second in line to the throne (his father, Prince Charles, is first in line), the wedding was not a full state occasion. This meant that the bride and groom could decide some of the details for themselves. Although there were many foreign royals, diplomats and state officials on the guest list, there were also very many of the couple's personal friends: around 1,900 guests were invited.

The procession was a grand affair with the use of state carriages and the Foot Guards and Household Cavalry taking part. The streets were lined with people hoping to catch a glimpse of the happy couple. After the ceremony, crowds gathered outside Buckingham Palace waiting for the Duke and Duchess of Cambridge to make an appearance on the balcony. They were not disappointed; the newlyweds appeared and delighted the crowds by kissing.

DID YOU KNOW?

More than 5,000 street parties were held in the United Kingdom. More than 1,000,000 people lined the route between Buckingham Palace and Westminster Abbey.

The Dress

Kate's wedding dress was designed by Sarah Burton who works for top designer label Alexander McQueen. The dress was much admired and retailers hurried to produce replicas that were on sale on the high street within days. Prince William wore an Irish Guards mounted officer's uniform.

Kate's Royal Tours

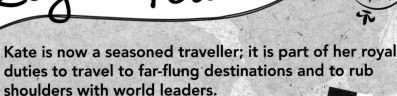

Kate is now a seasoned traveller; it is part of her royal duties to travel to far-flung destinations and to rub shoulders with world leaders.

Canada

Canada is a Commonwealth country and shares our royal family. In June 2011, just two months after they were married, the Duke and Duchess of Cambridge accepted an invitation from the government of Canada to undertake a **royal tour** of the country. The couple's visit took place between 30 June and 8 July 2011.

On their arrival in Ottawa, Kate and William laid a wreath at the Canadian Tomb of the Unknown Soldier at the Canadian National War Memorial. They were then officially welcomed by the Governor General, David Johnston. On their trip, Kate and William attended many functions, including a citizenship ceremony and they also unveiled a mural at the Canadian War Museum before taking a cooking lesson in Montreal!

The Duke of Cambridge's standard

The royal standard of Prince William, called the Duke of Cambridge's Personal Canadian Flag, has a shield of the Royal Arms of Canada. The flag was first used on the Royal Canadian Air Force plane that Prince William and Kate travelled on to Canada in 2011. It was unfurled from the cockpit window as the plane taxied after landing at Ottawa.

The United States of America

Straight after their tour of Canada, Kate and William flew to California, USA. They arrived in Los Angeles on 8 July and were whisked away to attend a technology conference in Beverley Hills. While in California, the couple played a game of polo in Santa Barbara, attended a glamorous **BAFTA awards** ceremony and visited an inner-city arts centre.

DID YOU KNOW?

Tuvalu is a tiny group of islands in the South Pacific.

The Duke and Duchess of Cambridge visit Kuala Lumpur, Malaysia (13 September 2012)

Singapore, Malaysia, Solomon Islands and Tuvalu

As a part of the Queen's Diamond Jubilee celebrations, Kate and William toured Singapore, Malaysia, Tuvalu and the Solomon Islands. During this overseas visit in September 2012, the Duchess made her first official speech abroad. When the couple visited the Solomon Islands, they wore grass skirts and took part in some traditional dancing. They were even carried on thrones when they arrived at Funafuti in Tuvalu!

The Royal Baby

There was much excitement in December 2012 when it was announced that the Duchess of Cambridge was pregnant with her first child. The eyes of the world were once again focused on Kate as people began to speculate on whether she would have a boy or a girl – and what name would be chosen for the future monarch.

The announcement of the royal pregnancy came earlier than the Duke and Duchess of Cambridge had originally planned. This is because Kate was admitted to hospital early on in her pregnancy suffering from severe **morning sickness**. Much to everyone's relief, she soon recovered. Concern became excitement as the nation began to anticipate the newest member of its royal family.

In a statement, St James's Palace said:

'Their Royal Highnesses the Duke and Duchess of Cambridge are very pleased to announce that the Duchess of Cambridge is expecting a baby.'

The statement went on to say:

'The Queen, the Duke of Edinburgh, the Prince of Wales, the Duchess of Cornwall and Prince Harry and members of both families are delighted with the news.'

Prince George
of Cambridge

was born on 22 July 2013.

He is third in line to the throne, after his grandfather, Prince Charles, and his father, Prince William.

Prince George was born in the Lindo Wing of St Mary's Hospital, Paddington, London – the same hospital where his father and his uncle, Prince Harry, were born. In the past, it has been custom for news of a royal birth to be first announced on an easel outside Buckingham Palace. However, the birth of Prince George was first announced in a press release by Palace officials, breaking with tradition.

People had been trying to guess whether the royal baby would be a boy or a girl. If the baby had been a girl, she would have made history. It used to be law that the first-born son of a monarch would be next in line to the throne over an older sister. This law was recently changed so that the first-born child of Kate and William would be next in line after William, whether the baby was a girl or a boy.

Princess at WORK

The life of a princess may seem like a glamorous one, but it is also very hard work. The Duke and Duchess of Cambridge receive an income from the Duchy of Cornwall and in return they carry out royal duties. The work they do, separately and together, promotes good causes and attracts millions of tourists to the UK every year.

The Duchess of Cambridge only took just over one month off from off from her royal duties after Prince George was born. She was soon back making public appearances.

On 30 August 2013, Kate made her first public appearance since the birth of Prince George. She attended the Anglesey ultra-marathon with her husband, who officially started the three-day, 220km (135-mile) coastal run. Anglesey is a special place for the couple as it was their home while Prince William worked as an RAF search and rescue helicopter pilot.

Kate has chosen to become a patron of many charities. Here are some of them:

The Art Room is a charity aimed at children with emotional and behavioural difficulties. It uses art workshops as a way to increase their confidence.

The National Portrait Gallery in London houses a collection of portraits of historically important and famous British people.

East Anglia's Children's Hospices (EACH) give care and support to children and young people with life-threatening illnesses, and their families.

Action on Addiction funds research into the problem of addiction to drink and drugs, and supports people in their efforts to fight it.

Place2Be gives support and counselling to troubled children in UK schools.

DID YOU KNOW?

Prince William's mother, Princess Diana, was also a patron of the Natural History Museum.

Sports Aid helps the sports stars of tomorrow by giving them cash awards to help pay for training at the start of their careers.

The Natural History Museum in London exhibits a vast range of specimens from the natural world.

Fashion
ICON

Kate has become something of a fashion icon and her down-to-earth attitude is admired by many. She often wears outfits from high-street retailers and is known for 'recycling' her red-carpet dresses, sometimes wearing them numerous times in public. Mostly, she is known for her graceful style and elegance.

Kate's fashion flair was noted by the media early in her public life. In 2006, she was selected by The *Daily Telegraph* as 'The most promising newcomer' in its list of style winners. By 2007, *Tatler* magazine had placed her at eighth on its yearly listing of top-ten style icons. In June 2008, *style.com* chose Kate as its beauty icon for that month, and in July 2008, Kate was included in *Vanity Fair*'s international best-dressed list. *Vanity Fair* placed Kate as number one in its annual best-dressed lists in 2010 and 2011. In 2012 she was also its 'cover star'.

Trend setter

Where Kate leads, others follow. When Kate visited a hospice wearing a cream coat with a Peter Pan collar from high-street store Topshop, the coat sold out across the nation as people rushed to buy a coat just like Kate's.

'The Duchess is an inspiration. She's very graceful, gracious and she's a brilliant ambassador for British fashion. She mixes up designer and high street; the perfect modern-day woman.'

Alice Temperley MBE, fashion designer

Favourite designers:

Jenny Packham
Alice Temperley
Alexander McQueen
Jimmy Choo
Roland Mouret
Stella McCartney

Favourite high-street stores:

Topshop
LK Bennet
Zara
Warehouse
Joseph
Reiss
Max Mara

27

How well do you know...

Kate, Duchess of Cambridge

The Duchess of Cambridge, or Kate, as she is still known by many, is often in the public eye. Test your knowledge to see how well you know her.

1 **What was Kate's favourite birthday memory?**
   a) Winning a game of pass the parcel
   b) A white rabbit cake made from marshmallows
   c) Eating an entire chocolate cake

2 **In which English county was Kate born?**
   a) Berkshire
   b) Yorkshire
   c) Buckinghamshire

3 **What is the name of Kate's family business?**
   a) Party On
   b) Celebration
   c) Party Pieces

4 **In which year did Kate and William first meet?**
   a) 1999
   b) 2001
   c) 2004

5 **Which university did Kate attend?**
   a) Oxford
   b) St Andrews, Fife
   c) Edinburgh

6 **What is Kate's middle name?**
   a) Elizabeth
   b) Victoria
   c) Albertina

7 **Who designed Kate's wedding dress?**
   a) Stella McCartney
   b) Topshop
   c) Sarah Burton at Alexander McQueen

8 What precious stones are in Kate's engagement ring?
a) Emeralds and pearls
b) A sapphire and diamonds
c) Rubies and diamonds

9 In which year did Kate marry Prince William?
a) 2012
b) 2009
c) 2011

10 What is the name of Kate and William's main residence?
a) Kensington Palace
b) Buckingham Palace
c) Windsor Castle

11 Which was the first country that Kate and William visited officially as a married couple?
a) Canada
b) Australia
c) Norway

12 What subject did Kate study at university?
a) Drama
b) Geography
c) History of Art

Answers

1. **b)** A white rabbit cake made from marshmallows
2. **a)** Berkshire
3. **c)** Party Pieces
4. **b)** 2001
5. **b)** St Andrews, Fife
6. **a)** Elizabeth
7. **c)** Sarah Burton at Alexander McQueen
8. **b)** A sapphire and diamonds
9. **c)** 2011
10. **a)** Kensington Palace
11. **a)** Canada
12. **c)** History of Art

Read all about her in these books:

Kate: *The Biography* by Marsha Moody published 2013 by Michael O'Mara Books Limited

Kate: *The Future Queen* by Katie Nicholl published 2013 by Weinstein Books

Kate's Style: *Smart, Chic Fashion from a Royal Role Model* by Caroline Jones published 2013 by Carlton Books Limited

You can find out more about Kate Middleton by logging on to:

http://www.royal.gov.uk/ThecurrentRoyalFamily/TheDuchessofCambridge/TheDuchessofCambridge.aspx

Quote sources

Page 7 The Daily Mail 2010; **Page 10** http://www.princeofwales.gov.uk/media/speeches/speech-hrh-the-duchess-of-cambridge-her-former-school-st-andrews-berkshire, 2012; **Page 12** The T3elegraph, 2005; **Page 13** The Daily Mail, 2011; **Page 14** The Daily Mail, 2010; **Page 15** The Telegraph, 2010; **Page 16** BBC, 2010; **Page 17** BBC, 2010; Page 21 The Daily Mail, 2013; **Page 24** St James' Palace official statement, 2012

Glossary

BAFTA awards
An awards ceremony given by the British Academy of Film and Television Arts

Chevron
A v-shaped pattern

Citizenship ceremony
A formal occasion at which people become citizens of their new country

Coat of arms
A crest that represents a family

Co-educational
Educating boys and girls together

Commonwealth
The Commonwealth of Nations (formerly, the British Commonwealth) is an organisation of territories that were mostly part of the former British Empire

Diplomats
Officials sent by a government to represent their country abroad

Duchy of Cornwall
Land held by the Duke of Cornwall

Dyslexic
A condition that makes it difficult to read and write

Environmental resources management
The management of ways in which humans can affect the environment

Flight attendant
An airline employee who is a member of the cabin crew and is responsible for the safety and comfort of the passengers on an aircraft

Flight dispatcher
An airline employee who plans flight paths

Merit
A good pass grade

Morning sickness
A condition suffered by some pregnant women

Palazzo Dello Strozzino
A grand old house in Florence, Italy, once owned by the Strozzi family

Patron
A person who supports a good cause by their effort or by giving money

Public relations
The management of information between a company or person and the public

Raleigh International
A UK youth organisation that promotes the environmentally-friendly development of our planet, formerly known as Operation Raleigh

Royal standard
The personal flag of a member of the royal family

Royal tour
A series of visits to different places by members of the royal family

Titled
Having a title, such as Lord or Lady, to show that you are of a high social class

Index